SCOTLAND
HIKING GUIDEBOOK
(2024 - 2025 EDITION)

Stella Melissa

Scotland Hiking Guidebook

Copyright © 2024 by Stella Melissa

All rights reserved. No part of this book may be reproduced, distributed, or transmitted in any form or by any means, including photocopying, recording, or other electronic or mechanical methods, without the prior written permission of the publisher, except in the case of brief quotations embodied in critical reviews and certain other noncommercial uses permitted by copyright law.

Stella Melissa

TABLE OF CONTENTS

INTRODUCTION

CHAPTER 1: DISCOVERING SCOTLAND
- Introduction to Scotland
- Brief History and Culture
- Why Hike in Scotland?
- Quick Facts about Scotland

CHAPTER 2: PLANNING YOUR TRIP
- Best Time to Hike
- Entry Fees and Permits
- Historic Sites and Managed Trails
- Accommodation Options
- Practical Tips for Booking Accommodation

CHAPTER 3: TOP HIKING DESTINATIONS
- Must-Hike Trails
- The Great Glen Way
- National Parks and Natural Reserves

- Loch Lomond and The Trossachs National Park
- Iconic Mountains and Peaks
- Coastal and Island Hikes
- Hidden Gems: Lesser-Known Trails
- Practical Tips for Hiking in Scotland

CHAPTER 4: CULTURAL AND HISTORICAL INSIGHTS

- Scotland's Rich History
- Traditions and Customs
- Festivals and Events Along the Trails

CHAPTER 5: GETTING AROUND SCOTLAND

- Transportation Options
- Navigating Hiking Trails: Maps and Apps
- Driving in Scotland: Tips and Regulations
- Recommended Hiking Itineraries

CHAPTER 6: FOOD AND DRINK

- Introduction to Scottish Cuisine

Stella Melissa

- Must-Try Dishes and Local Specialties
- Best Places to Eat and Drink on Your Hike
- Food Markets and Culinary Tours
- Traditional Pubs and Whisky Trails
- Tips for Enjoying Scottish Food and Drink

CHAPTER 7: PRACTICAL INFORMATION AND TRAVEL TIPS

- Internet and Communication
- Money Matters: Currency, ATMs, and Tipping
- Local Etiquette
- Sustainable and Responsible Hiking
- Essential Gear and Packing Checklist

APPENDICES

- 15 FAQs About Hiking in Scotland
- 15 Fun Facts About Scotland
- Emergency Contacts and Useful Links

MAP OF SCOTTISH HIGHLAND

Scotland Hiking Guidebook

INTRODUCTION

Welcome, fellow adventurer, to the heart of Scotland! Allow me to paint you a vivid picture of this mystical land, where ancient legends dance with the whispers of the wind, and every path you tread leads to a story waiting to be told. As you hold this guidebook in your hands, I am brimming with excitement to share my experiences, hoping to inspire you to embark on your own Scottish journey.

Imagine waking up to the crisp morning air, the scent of dew-kissed heather mingling with the earthy aroma of ancient pine forests. The sun peeks over the horizon, casting a golden hue over rolling hills and dramatic mountain ranges. This is Scotland, where every sunrise feels like a grand unveiling of nature's splendor.

I remember my first hike in the Scottish Highlands as if it were yesterday. The trail led me through the enchanting Glen Coe, often referred to as the "Glen of Weeping." Despite its melancholic name, the valley's

Stella Melissa

beauty was anything but sorrowful. Towering peaks framed my path, their rugged silhouettes softened by the morning mist. As I ventured deeper, I stumbled upon a hidden waterfall, its cascading waters sparkling like liquid diamonds in the sunlight. There, surrounded by nature's raw beauty, I felt a profound connection to the land, as if the spirits of ancient clans were guiding my steps.

One cannot speak of Scotland without mentioning its legendary lochs. Picture yourself standing on the shores of Loch Ness, the mysterious waters stretching out before you. The air is thick with anticipation, and you can't help but scan the surface for a glimpse of the elusive Nessie. While the legendary creature remained a mystery during my visit, the sheer majesty of the loch and its surrounding landscape left me in awe. The tranquility of the water, mirrored by the serene sky, creates a perfect backdrop for contemplation and wonder.

Scotland Hiking Guidebook

As you traverse the varied terrains of Scotland, you'll encounter charming villages where time seems to stand still. One such gem is the village of Dunkeld, nestled on the banks of the River Tay. Wandering through its narrow streets, I discovered quaint cottages adorned with vibrant flower boxes, and the sweet melody of a fiddle drifted from a local pub. The warmth and hospitality of the villagers made me feel like I had found a home away from home. Over a hearty meal of haggis and tatties, I listened to tales of ancient battles and folklore, each story weaving a rich tapestry of Scotland's history.

Scotland's trails are not just about the destination, but the journey itself. I recall a particularly exhilarating hike up Ben Nevis, the highest peak in the British Isles. The ascent was challenging, but every step was rewarded with breathtaking vistas of glacial valleys and emerald-green pastures. Reaching the summit, I was greeted by a panoramic view that seemed to stretch to the edge of the world. In that moment, I understood why so many before me had been drawn to this rugged and unyielding

Stella Melissa

landscape.

But Scotland is not only for the seasoned hiker; it welcomes all who seek to explore its wonders. Whether you're wandering through the mystical forests of the Trossachs, marveling at the ancient standing stones of the Isle of Skye, or simply enjoying a leisurely stroll along the sandy beaches of Arisaig, Scotland offers a myriad of experiences to suit every adventurer's heart.

As you delve into this guidebook, let my stories ignite your imagination and fuel your desire to explore Scotland's untamed beauty. Within these pages, you'll find detailed trail descriptions, practical tips, and hidden gems that will help you navigate this extraordinary land with ease and confidence. So lace up your hiking boots, pack your sense of adventure, and get ready to embark on a journey that will leave you with memories to cherish for a lifetime.

Welcome to Scotland, my friend. The adventure of a lifetime awaits you.

Scotland Hiking Guidebook

CHAPTER 1: DISCOVERING SCOTLAND

Introduction to Scotland

Welcome to Scotland, a land where ancient history meets vibrant modernity, where rugged landscapes blend seamlessly with picturesque villages, and where every corner holds a story waiting to be discovered. Scotland, the northernmost country of the United Kingdom, is a place of striking natural beauty and deep cultural heritage. From its rolling Highlands and serene lochs to its bustling cities and charming coastal towns, Scotland offers a diverse array of experiences for every traveler.

Nestled between the North Sea and the Atlantic Ocean, Scotland's geography is as varied as it is breathtaking. The country is divided into three main regions: the Highlands, the Central Belt, and the Southern Uplands. The Highlands are famous for their dramatic mountain ranges, including the Grampian Mountains and the Northwest Highlands, while the Central Belt is home to Scotland's two largest cities, Edinburgh and Glasgow. The Southern Uplands, with their gentle hills and fertile valleys, provide a more pastoral landscape.

Scotland's climate is temperate, characterized by cool summers and mild winters. While the weather can be unpredictable, it is this very unpredictability that adds to the charm of the Scottish outdoors. Misty mornings give way to sunlit afternoons, and the ever-changing skies create a dynamic backdrop for any adventure.

equally dynamic, with bands like The Proclaimers and Franz Ferdinand gaining international acclaim.

Scottish cuisine is hearty and rooted in local produce. From the famous haggis to the simple delight of freshly caught seafood, Scotland offers a culinary experience that is both unique and satisfying. The country's whisky, often referred to as "liquid gold," is world-famous, with distilleries dotting the landscape and offering tours and tastings to visitors.

Why Hike in Scotland?

Hiking in Scotland is not just an activity; it is an immersive experience that connects you with the land's natural beauty, history, and culture. There are countless reasons to lace up your hiking boots and explore Scotland's trails, whether you are an experienced hiker or a newcomer to the world of outdoor adventure.

1. Stunning Landscapes: Scotland's landscapes are some of the most breathtaking in the world. The rugged peaks

Stella Melissa

of the Highlands, the serene beauty of the lochs, the dramatic coastlines, and the rolling hills of the Lowlands all offer diverse and captivating scenery. Each hike presents a new vista, from the sweeping glens to the heather-covered moorlands.

2. Rich History: Hiking in Scotland allows you to walk in the footsteps of history. Many trails pass by ancient ruins, castles, and battlefields, offering a glimpse into the country's storied past. The sense of connection to those who have walked these paths before is both humbling and inspiring.

3. Wildlife: Scotland is home to a wide variety of wildlife. As you hike, you may encounter red deer, golden eagles, otters, and even the elusive Scottish wildcat. The coastal areas are a haven for seabirds, seals, and dolphins. The opportunity to observe these creatures in their natural habitat adds a thrilling dimension to any hike.

4. Accessibility: Scotland boasts a well-maintained network of trails suitable for all levels of experience. Whether you are looking for a challenging multi-day trek or a leisurely day hike, you will find a route that matches your abilities and interests. The right to roam, enshrined in Scottish law, allows you to explore the countryside freely, ensuring that you can truly immerse yourself in the landscape.

5. Cultural Experience: Hiking in Scotland is not just about the natural environment; it is also an opportunity to engage with the local culture. Small villages and towns along the trails offer a warm welcome, traditional hospitality, and a chance to experience Scottish life up close. Enjoying a hearty meal in a local pub after a day of hiking or participating in a ceilidh dance are experiences that enrich your journey.

6. Health and Well-being: The physical benefits of hiking are well-documented, from improved cardiovascular health to increased strength and stamina. However, the mental and emotional benefits are equally

significant. The tranquility of the Scottish countryside, the fresh air, and the sense of accomplishment that comes from reaching your destination all contribute to a sense of well-being and happiness.

Quick Facts about Scotland

To help you get acquainted with Scotland, here are some quick facts that provide a snapshot of this remarkable country:

- Location: Scotland is part of the United Kingdom, located in the northern part of the island of Great Britain.
- Capital: Edinburgh, known for its historic and cultural attractions, including the famous Edinburgh Castle and the annual Edinburgh Festival.
- Largest City: Glasgow, a vibrant city renowned for its music scene, art galleries, and friendly locals.
- Population: Approximately 5.5 million people.
- Language: The official languages are English, Scots, and Scottish Gaelic. Gaelic is primarily spoken in the Highlands and the Western Isles.

Scotland Hiking Guidebook

- Currency: Pound Sterling (£).

- Government: Scotland has its own parliament and operates under a devolved system of government within the United Kingdom.

- Climate: The climate is temperate maritime, characterized by mild temperatures and frequent rainfall. Weather can be highly variable, with rapid changes common.

- National Symbols: The thistle is the national flower, and the unicorn is the national animal. The Saltire (St. Andrew's Cross) is the national flag.

- Whisky: Scotland is famous for its whisky, with over 130 active distilleries. Each region produces whisky with distinct characteristics, from the peaty Islay malts to the smooth Speyside whiskies.

- Festivals: Scotland hosts numerous festivals throughout the year, including the Edinburgh Festival Fringe, the largest arts festival in the world, and Hogmanay, the traditional New Year celebration.

- UNESCO World Heritage Sites: Scotland is home to six UNESCO World Heritage Sites, including the Heart of Neolithic Orkney and the Old and New Towns of Edinburgh.

- Famous Landmarks: Iconic landmarks include Loch Ness, home of the legendary Loch Ness Monster; the Isle of Skye, known for its rugged beauty; and the historic Stirling Castle.

As you embark on your journey through this guidebook, let these insights and stories inspire your own adventure. Scotland awaits, with its wild landscapes, rich history, and warm-hearted people ready to welcome you to a land of endless discovery. Whether you are here for the towering mountains, the tranquil lochs, or the ancient ruins, you will find that Scotland offers a hiking experience unlike any other. So, prepare yourself for an unforgettable journey into the heart of this remarkable country.

Scotland Hiking Guidebook

CHAPTER 2: PLANNING YOUR TRIP

Best Time to Hike

Scotland's diverse landscapes offer hiking opportunities year-round, but the best time to hike largely depends on your preferences for weather, daylight, and crowds.

Spring (March to May)

Spring in Scotland is a magical time. As the snow melts, the landscapes burst into life with blooming wildflowers and lush greenery. Temperatures are moderate, ranging from 5°C to 15°C (41°F to 59°F), making it comfortable for hiking. Daylight extends to about 10-14 hours, giving you ample time to explore. However, be prepared for unpredictable weather, including occasional rain showers.

Highlights:
- Wildflowers in full bloom
- Fewer tourists compared to summer
- Ideal for photographing landscapes

Summer (June to August)

Summer is the most popular time for hiking in Scotland. With temperatures ranging from 10°C to 20°C (50°F to 68°F), it's perfect for outdoor activities. Daylight lasts up to 18 hours, allowing for extended hikes. However, this is also the peak tourist season, so expect busier trails and higher accommodation prices. Additionally, midges (tiny biting insects) can be a nuisance in the Highlands and western Scotland.

Scotland Hiking Guidebook

Highlights:
- Long daylight hours
- Warmer temperatures
- Festivals and events in local villages

Autumn (September to November)

Autumn is a fantastic time for hiking, with cooler temperatures between 5°C to 15°C (41°F to 59°F) and stunning fall foliage. The trails are less crowded, and the weather is generally stable, though it can be unpredictable towards November. Daylight hours start to shorten, ranging from 9-12 hours.

Highlights:
- Vibrant autumn colors
- Quieter trails
- Cooler hiking conditions

Winter (December to February)

Stella Melissa

Winter hiking in Scotland is for the more adventurous. Temperatures can drop below freezing, especially in the mountains, and daylight is limited to about 6-8 hours. Snow and ice are common, making some trails challenging or inaccessible without proper equipment and experience. However, the winter landscapes are breathtakingly beautiful, and there's a unique tranquility to be found.

Highlights:
- Snow-covered landscapes
- Peaceful and serene environment
- Opportunities for winter sports

Entry Fees and Permits

National Parks and Nature Reserves

Scotland is home to two national parks: Cairngorms National Park and Loch Lomond and The Trossachs National Park. Both parks offer extensive hiking trails and natural beauty, and entry to these parks is free.

However, some specific activities or areas within these parks might require permits or fees.

Cairngorms National Park
- Entry: Free
- Activities: Some activities like fishing and certain guided tours may require a permit.
- Contact Information:
  - Address: 14 The Square, Grantown-on-Spey, PH26 3HG, Scotland
  - Phone: +44 1479 873535
  - Website: [Cairngorms National Park](https://cairngorms.co.uk)

Loch Lomond and The Trossachs National Park
- Entry: Free
- Activities: Camping in designated areas may require a permit.
- Contact Information:
  - Address: Carrochan, Carrochan Road, Balloch, G83 8EG, Scotland
  - Phone: +44 1389 722600

Stella Melissa

- Website: [Loch Lomond and The Trossachs](https://www.lochlomond-trossachs.org)

Historic Sites and Managed Trails

Some historic sites and managed trails may have entry fees or require permits. It's advisable to check the specific requirements for each location you plan to visit.

 Example: Ben Nevis
- Entry: Free
- Parking: £4 per day at Glen Nevis Visitor Centre car park
- Contact Information:
  - Address: Glen Nevis Visitor Centre, Glen Nevis, Fort William, PH33 6PF, Scotland
  - Phone: +44 1397 705922
  - Website: [Ben Nevis](https://www.outdoorcapital.co.uk/ben-nevis/)

Accommodation Options

When planning your hiking trip to Scotland, finding the right accommodation is crucial for a comfortable and enjoyable experience. Scotland offers a variety of options, from campgrounds and lodges to hotels. Here are some real samples of accommodation options in and around popular hiking areas.

Campgrounds

Glen Nevis Caravan and Camping Park
Located near Fort William, this campground is an ideal base for hiking Ben Nevis and exploring the surrounding area.

- Address: Glen Nevis, Fort William, PH33 6SX, Scotland
- Contact: +44 1397 702191
- Website: [Glen Nevis Caravan and Camping Park](https://www.glen-nevis.co.uk)

Stella Melissa

- Facilities: Tent pitches, caravan sites, shower facilities, laundry, on-site shop

Rothiemurchus Camp and Caravan Park
Nestled in the Cairngorms National Park, this campground offers a serene setting for outdoor enthusiasts.

- Address: Coylumbridge, Aviemore, PH22 1QU, Scotland
- Contact: +44 1479 812800
- Website: [Rothiemurchus Camp and Caravan Park](https://rothiemurchus.net)
- Facilities: Tent pitches, caravan sites, hot showers, communal kitchen, Wi-Fi

Lodges

The Sligachan Hotel
Located on the Isle of Skye, The Sligachan Hotel offers comfortable lodging with stunning views of the Cuillin mountains.

- Address: Sligachan, Isle of Skye, IV47 8SW, Scotland
- Contact: +44 1478 650204
- Website: [The Sligachan Hotel](https://www.sligachan.co.uk)
- Facilities: En-suite rooms, restaurant, bar, Wi-Fi, free parking

Glenmore Lodge

Scotland's National Outdoor Training Centre, Glenmore Lodge in Aviemore, offers both accommodation and training courses for outdoor activities.

- Address: Aviemore, PH22 1QU, Scotland
- Contact: +44 1479 861256
- Website: [Glenmore Lodge](https://www.glenmorelodge.org.uk)
- Facilities: En-suite rooms, self-catering apartments, on-site restaurant, gear rental

Hotels

The Torridon

Stella Melissa

A luxury hotel set in the heart of the Highlands, The Torridon provides a lavish stay with easy access to numerous hiking trails.

- Address: Torridon, By Achnasheen, Wester Ross, IV22 2EY, Scotland
- Contact: +44 1445 791242
- Website: [The Torridon](https://www.thetorridon.com)
- Facilities: Luxury rooms, fine dining, bar, outdoor activities, spa services

The Balmoral Hotel

Located in Edinburgh, The Balmoral Hotel offers a luxurious retreat with convenient access to urban hikes and historical sites.

- Address: 1 Princes St, Edinburgh, EH2 2EQ, Scotland
- Contact: +44 131 556 2414
- Website: [The Balmoral Hotel](https://www.roccofortehotels.com/hotels-and-resorts/the-balmoral-hotel)

- Facilities: Luxury rooms and suites, Michelin-starred restaurant, bar, spa, fitness center

Practical Tips for Booking Accommodation

1. Book in Advance: Popular hiking areas can get crowded, especially during peak seasons. Booking your accommodation well in advance ensures you have a place to stay and can often get better rates.

2. Check Reviews: Websites like TripAdvisor and Booking.com offer reviews from previous guests. Reading these can provide insights into the quality and services of the accommodation.

3. Consider Location: Choose accommodation that is conveniently located near your planned hiking trails. This reduces travel time and allows you to maximize your time exploring.

4. Look for Amenities: Depending on your needs, look for amenities such as Wi-Fi, laundry facilities, and on-

site dining options. For camping, check for essential facilities like showers and cooking areas.

5. Be Prepared for Weather: Scotland's weather can be unpredictable. Ensure your accommodation is equipped to handle the elements, whether it's heating for cold nights or secure storage for wet gear.

6. Local Knowledge: Hosts and staff at local accommodations can often provide valuable advice on hiking trails, weather conditions, and must-see spots. Don't hesitate to ask for recommendations.

By carefully planning the timing of your trip, understanding entry fees and permits, and selecting the right accommodation, you'll set the foundation for an unforgettable hiking adventure in Scotland. Let this guide be your companion as you prepare to explore the breathtaking landscapes and rich heritage of this extraordinary country.

Scotland Hiking Guidebook

CHAPTER 3: TOP HIKING DESTINATIONS

Scotland is a hiker's paradise, offering an array of stunning landscapes, from majestic mountains and serene lochs to rugged coastlines and mystical forests. In this chapter, we delve into the top hiking destinations across the country, each providing unique experiences and breathtaking views. We'll explore must-hike trails, national parks, iconic mountains, coastal and island hikes, and hidden gems that promise to delight every adventurer.

Stella Melissa

Must-Hike Trails

West Highland Way

Overview:
The West Highland Way is Scotland's most famous long-distance trail, stretching 96 miles (154 kilometers) from Milngavie, just outside Glasgow, to Fort William in the Highlands. This trail offers a diverse range of landscapes, including lochs, moorlands, and towering mountains.

Location:
- Start: Milngavie, East Dunbartonshire
- End: Fort William, Highland

History:
Established in 1980, the West Highland Way was Scotland's first official long-distance footpath. It follows ancient drovers' roads, military roads, and old coaching routes, offering hikers a journey through Scotland's rich history and scenic beauty.

Visiting Hours:

The trail is open year-round, but the best time to hike is from April to October, when the weather is more favorable, and services along the route are fully operational.

Restrictions:

- Camping: Wild camping is allowed, but campers must follow the Scottish Outdoor Access Code.
- Dogs: Dogs are allowed but should be kept under control, especially around livestock.

The Great Glen Way

Overview:

The Great Glen Way spans 79 miles (127 kilometers) from Fort William to Inverness, following the natural fault line that divides the Highlands. The trail takes hikers along the Caledonian Canal and the shores of Loch Ness, offering a mix of woodland, canal paths, and open countryside.

Stella Melissa

Location:
- Start: Fort William, Highland
- End: Inverness, Highland

History:
Opened in 2002, the Great Glen Way was designed to provide a scenic and accessible route through one of Scotland's most significant geological features. It connects with the West Highland Way, offering an extended hiking adventure for those who wish to explore further.

Visiting Hours:
The trail is accessible year-round, with the peak hiking season from April to October.

Restrictions:
- Camping: Designated camping areas are available, and wild camping is permitted with adherence to the Scottish Outdoor Access Code.
- Dogs: Allowed but must be controlled around livestock.

Scotland Hiking Guidebook

National Parks and Natural Reserves

Cairngorms National Park

Overview:

Cairngorms National Park, the largest national park in the UK, is a haven for outdoor enthusiasts. It features rugged mountains, ancient forests, and diverse wildlife, offering numerous hiking opportunities for all levels.

Location:
- Region: Northeast Scotland
- Nearest Towns: Aviemore, Braemar, Grantown-on-Spey

History:

Established in 2003, Cairngorms National Park was created to protect the unique landscapes and biodiversity of the region. The park encompasses five of the UK's highest mountains and several nature reserves.

Visiting Hours:

Stella Melissa

The park is open year-round, with visitor centers providing information on trails, wildlife, and weather conditions.

Restrictions:
- Camping: Permitted in designated areas and wild camping is allowed following the Scottish Outdoor Access Code.
- Dogs: Allowed but must be kept on a lead during bird nesting season and around livestock.

Loch Lomond and The Trossachs National Park

Overview:
Loch Lomond and The Trossachs National Park is renowned for its stunning lochs, rolling hills, and scenic glens. It offers a variety of hiking trails, from leisurely walks to challenging climbs.

Location:
- Region: Central Scotland

Scotland Hiking Guidebook

- Nearest Towns: Balloch, Callander, Aberfoyle

History:
Established in 2002, this park aims to preserve the natural beauty and cultural heritage of the area. It includes the famous Loch Lomond, the largest inland stretch of water in Great Britain.

Visiting Hours:
The park is accessible year-round, with visitor centers providing maps, guides, and safety information.

Restrictions:
- Camping: Designated camping areas are available, and wild camping is permitted under the Scottish Outdoor Access Code.
- Dogs: Allowed but should be kept on a lead near livestock and during the bird nesting season.

Iconic Mountains and Peaks

Ben Nevis

Stella Melissa

Overview:

Ben Nevis, the highest mountain in the British Isles, stands at 1,345 meters (4,413 feet) above sea level. It is a magnet for hikers and climbers, offering breathtaking views from its summit.

Location:

- Region: Highland
- Nearest Town: Fort William

History:

Ben Nevis, known locally as "The Ben," is part of the Grampian Mountain range and has a rich geological and climbing history. The mountain's name is derived from the Gaelic words meaning "venomous mountain" or "mountain with its head in the clouds."

Visiting Hours:

Ben Nevis can be climbed year-round, but the best time is from late spring to early autumn. Winter ascents require experience and proper equipment.

Restrictions:
- Camping: Permitted in designated areas and wild camping is allowed.
- Dogs: Allowed but must be controlled, especially near livestock and in the summit area.

Schiehallion

Overview:
Schiehallion, also known as the "Fairy Hill of the Caledonians," is one of Scotland's most iconic Munros, standing at 1,083 meters (3,553 feet). It offers a relatively accessible hike with rewarding panoramic views.

Location:
- Region: Perth and Kinross
- Nearest Town: Kinloch Rannoch

History:
Schiehallion is famous for the 18th-century experiment conducted by Charles Hutton to estimate the Earth's

mass. The mountain's symmetrical shape made it ideal for this scientific endeavor.

Visiting Hours:
The mountain can be hiked year-round, but the best conditions are from late spring to early autumn.

Restrictions:
- Camping: Wild camping is allowed, following the Scottish Outdoor Access Code.
- Dogs: Allowed but should be kept on a lead near wildlife and livestock.

Coastal and Island Hikes

Isle of Skye: The Quiraing

Overview:
The Quiraing on the Isle of Skye is a dramatic landslip providing some of the most stunning and otherworldly landscapes in Scotland. The trail offers unique rock formations, cliffs, and panoramic views over the island.

Location:
- Region: Isle of Skye
- Nearest Village: Staffin

History:
The Quiraing is part of the Trotternish Ridge and has been shaped by centuries of landslides. Its unique geological features make it a favorite among photographers and hikers.

Visiting Hours:
The trail is open year-round, but the best time to visit is from late spring to early autumn.

Restrictions:
- Camping: Wild camping is permitted under the Scottish Outdoor Access Code.
- Dogs: Allowed but must be kept on a lead around livestock.

Fife Coastal Path

Stella Melissa

Overview:

The Fife Coastal Path stretches 117 miles (188 kilometers) along the picturesque coastline of Fife, offering diverse landscapes from sandy beaches to rugged cliffs and charming fishing villages.

Location:

- Region: Fife
- Nearest Towns: North Queensferry, St Andrews

History:

Established in 2002, the Fife Coastal Path connects historic sites, nature reserves, and coastal communities, providing a scenic and cultural hiking experience.

Visiting Hours:

The path is accessible year-round, with each season offering unique attractions.

Restrictions:

- Camping: Designated camping areas are available, and wild camping is allowed.

- Dogs: Allowed but should be kept on a lead in nature reserves and around livestock.

Hidden Gems: Lesser-Known Trails

The Falls of Glomach

Overview:
The Falls of Glomach is one of the highest waterfalls in Britain, located in a remote area of the Northwest Highlands. The hike to the falls offers solitude and stunning natural beauty.

Location:
- Region: Highland
- Nearest Village: Dornie

History:
The falls drop 113 meters (370 feet) and are set within a dramatic, narrow cleft. The remote location adds to the sense of adventure for those who make the trek.

Visiting Hours:
The trail is open year-round, but the best time to visit is from late spring to early autumn.

Restrictions:
- Camping: Wild camping is allowed, following the Scottish Outdoor Access Code.
- Dogs: Allowed but must be controlled around wildlife.

Sandwood Bay

Overview:
Sandwood Bay is a pristine beach in the far northwest of Scotland, known for its golden sands and dramatic sea stacks. The hike to the bay offers a remote and untouched coastal experience.

Location:
- Region: Sutherland
- Nearest Village: Kinlochbervie

History:

Sandwood Bay has a sense of mystery and legend, including tales of shipwrecks and mermaids. It is considered one of the most beautiful and unspoiled beaches in Britain.

Visiting Hours:
Accessible year-round, though the best conditions are in late spring to early autumn.

Restrictions:
- Camping: Wild camping is allowed, adhering to the Scottish Outdoor Access Code.
- Dogs: Allowed but should be kept on a lead around wildlife.

Practical Tips for Hiking in Scotland

Weather and Gear

Scotland's weather can be unpredictable, so it's essential to be prepared for all conditions. Always check the weather forecast before heading out and dress in layers.

Waterproof clothing and sturdy hiking boots are a must. A good map, compass, and GPS device are also recommended, especially for remote areas.

Safety and Etiquette

- Leave No Trace: Follow the Scottish Outdoor Access Code by respecting wildlife, taking your litter home, and leaving the natural environment as you found it.
- Stay on Trails: Stick to marked paths to minimize erosion and protect the environment.
- Respect Wildlife and Livestock: Keep a safe distance from animals and close gates behind you.
- Emergency Services: Dial 999 or 112 for emergency assistance. It's also advisable to inform someone of your hiking plans and expected return time.

Local Culture and Traditions

Scotland is rich in culture and traditions, and respecting local customs enhances your experience. Learn a few Gaelic phrases, try local foods, and participate in community events when possible. Scottish hospitality is renowned, and engaging with locals can provide deeper insights into the places you visit.

Scotland's hiking trails offer an unparalleled blend of natural beauty, history, and adventure. From iconic peaks and serene lochs to rugged coastlines and hidden gems, there's something for every hiker. As you plan your journey, let this guide be your companion, providing you with the information and inspiration needed to explore Scotland with confidence and awe.

CHAPTER 4: CULTURAL AND HISTORICAL INSIGHTS

Scotland's hiking trails are not only routes through stunning landscapes but also pathways through a rich tapestry of history and culture. From ancient clans and battles to vibrant festivals and unique customs, every step you take in Scotland is steeped in stories waiting to be discovered. In this chapter, we will delve into Scotland's rich history, explore its traditions and customs, and highlight the festivals and events you might encounter along the trails.

Scotland's Rich History

Ancient Scotland

Prehistoric Times:
Scotland's history dates back thousands of years, with evidence of human habitation as far back as 12,000 years ago. The Mesolithic period saw the first hunter-gatherers, who left behind tools and settlements that

provide a glimpse into their lives. Sites like Skara Brae in Orkney, a well-preserved Neolithic village, offer fascinating insights into early Scottish life.

Roman Influence:
The Romans made their mark on Scotland, though they never fully conquered the region. Hadrian's Wall, built in the early 2nd century AD, marks the northern limit of the Roman Empire and stands as a testament to their efforts to control the area. The Antonine Wall, a lesser-known Roman frontier, also stretches across central Scotland.

Medieval Scotland

The Picts and the Scots:
In the early medieval period, Scotland was home to the Picts and the Scots, two distinct groups with their own cultures and territories. The unification of these groups in the 9th century under Kenneth MacAlpin laid the foundation for the Kingdom of Scotland.

The Wars of Independence:

Stella Melissa

The late 13th and early 14th centuries were marked by the Wars of Independence against England. Figures like William Wallace and Robert the Bruce became national heroes. The Battle of Bannockburn in 1314, where Robert the Bruce secured a significant victory, is a key event in Scottish history.

The Stuart Dynasty

The Rise of the Stuarts:
The Stuart dynasty began with Robert II in the 14th century and saw Scotland flourish culturally and politically. Mary, Queen of Scots, is one of the most famous Stuarts, known for her tumultuous life and tragic end.

Union with England:
The Union of the Crowns in 1603 brought Scotland and England under a single monarch, James VI of Scotland, who became James I of England. The subsequent Act of Union in 1707 merged the two countries into the

Kingdom of Great Britain, a contentious decision that still sparks debate today.

Modern Scotland

Industrial Revolution:
The 18th and 19th centuries saw Scotland play a crucial role in the Industrial Revolution. Cities like Glasgow and Edinburgh became centers of innovation and industry, contributing significantly to advancements in engineering, medicine, and the arts.

Devolution:
In recent history, the establishment of the Scottish Parliament in 1999 marked a significant step towards greater autonomy for Scotland. The ongoing discussions about independence continue to shape the nation's political landscape.

Traditions and Customs

Highland Games

Stella Melissa

Overview:

The Highland Games are a quintessential Scottish tradition, showcasing the country's athleticism, music, and dance. These events, held throughout the summer, feature traditional sports such as caber tossing, hammer throwing, and tug-of-war, accompanied by bagpipe music and Highland dancing.

History:

The origins of the Highland Games are believed to date back to the 11th century, during the reign of King Malcolm III, who used them to recruit the strongest men for his army. Today, they celebrate Scottish heritage and bring communities together.

Ceilidh Dancing

Overview:

A ceilidh (pronounced kay-lee) is a traditional Scottish social gathering featuring lively folk music and dancing. These events are a staple of Scottish culture, often held in village halls, community centers, and during festivals.

History:
Ceilidhs have their roots in Gaelic culture and were originally gatherings for storytelling, poetry, and music. Over time, dancing became a central element, with traditional reels, jigs, and strathspeys performed to the tunes of fiddles and accordions.

Tartan and Kilts

Overview:
Tartan, a patterned cloth with crisscrossed horizontal and vertical bands in multiple colors, is synonymous with Scottish identity. Kilts, made from tartan fabric, are traditional garments worn by men and women, especially during formal occasions and cultural events.

History:
Tartans have been used in Scotland for centuries, with each clan historically having its own unique pattern. The kilt, as we know it today, evolved from the great kilt, a large piece of tartan cloth worn in the 16th century. It

became a symbol of Scottish pride and heritage, especially after the Jacobite uprisings.

Haggis and Scottish Cuisine

Overview:
Haggis is Scotland's national dish, made from sheep's offal mixed with oatmeal, suet, and spices, traditionally encased in the animal's stomach. It is often served with "neeps and tatties" (turnips and potatoes) and enjoyed during Burns Night celebrations.

History:
The origins of haggis are ancient, with similar dishes found in various cultures. However, it became particularly associated with Scotland in the 18th century. Burns Night, celebrated on January 25th in honor of poet Robert Burns, is a key event where haggis takes center stage.

Festivals and Events Along the Trails

The Edinburgh Festival Fringe

Overview:
The Edinburgh Festival Fringe is the world's largest arts festival, held annually in August. It features thousands of performances spanning comedy, theater, dance, music, and more, attracting artists and audiences from around the globe.

Location:
- City: Edinburgh

Highlights:
- Street Performances: The Royal Mile transforms into a bustling hub of street performers.
- Comedy and Theater: Renowned for launching the careers of many famous comedians and actors.
- International Acts: A diverse range of performances from different cultures and genres.

Stella Melissa

The Royal Edinburgh Military Tattoo

Overview:

The Royal Edinburgh Military Tattoo is a spectacular display of military music, dance, and precision, held annually in August against the backdrop of Edinburgh Castle. It features performers from across the world, showcasing their unique cultural traditions.

Location:
- City: Edinburgh
- Venue: Edinburgh Castle Esplanade

Highlights:
- Massed Pipes and Drums: A stirring performance by military bands from around the globe.
- Cultural Performances: Dance and music acts from various countries.
- Fireworks: Nightly fireworks displays lighting up the Edinburgh skyline.

Hogmanay

Scotland Hiking Guidebook

Overview:

Hogmanay is Scotland's New Year celebration, renowned for its vibrant street parties, fireworks, and traditions. Edinburgh's Hogmanay is the most famous, attracting visitors worldwide to ring in the new year with festivities.

Location:

- City: Edinburgh (main event), with celebrations across Scotland

Highlights:

- Torchlight Procession: A stunning procession through Edinburgh's streets, culminating in a fireworks display.
- Street Party: Live music, dancing, and celebrations in the heart of the city.
- Loony Dook: A traditional New Year's Day dip in the freezing waters of the River Forth.

Beltane Fire Festival

Overview:

Stella Melissa

The Beltane Fire Festival is an annual celebration of the ancient Celtic festival of Beltane, marking the beginning of summer. Held on April 30th, it features fire displays, music, and performances inspired by Celtic mythology.

Location:
- City: Edinburgh
- Venue: Calton Hill

Highlights:
- Fire Processions: Torchbearers and fire performers creating a magical spectacle.
- Mythological Characters: Performers embodying figures from Celtic mythology.
- Dance and Music: Traditional and contemporary performances celebrating the arrival of summer.

Orkney Folk Festival

Overview:
The Orkney Folk Festival is a celebration of traditional Scottish music, held annually in May in the Orkney

Islands. It brings together local and international musicians for a weekend of concerts, ceilidhs, and workshops.

Location:
- Region: Orkney Islands
- Main Town: Stromness

Highlights:
- Concerts: Performances by renowned folk artists and emerging talent.
- Ceilidhs: Traditional dance events open to all.
- Workshops: Opportunities to learn about folk music and instruments.

The Braemar Gathering

Overview:
The Braemar Gathering is one of the most famous Highland Games events, held annually on the first Saturday in September. It is attended by members of the

British Royal Family and features traditional Highland sports, music, and dance.

Location:
- Village: Braemar
- Region: Aberdeenshire

Highlights:
- Caber Tossing: One of the signature events, showcasing strength and skill.
- Piping Competitions: Featuring some of the best bagpipers in the world.
- Highland Dancing: Traditional dances performed in vibrant attire.

Scotland's trails offer more than just physical challenges and stunning vistas; they provide a journey through the heart of Scottish culture and history. As you hike through this magnificent country, you'll encounter ancient ruins, traditional music, and lively festivals that bring Scotland's rich heritage to life. Embrace the opportunity to immerse yourself in these cultural and historical insights, and you'll find that every step you take on Scotland's paths is a step into a story that has been unfolding for millennia. Whether it's the tales of ancient clans, the sound of bagpipes echoing through the glens, or the taste of haggis at a local festival, Scotland's trails promise an unforgettable adventure steeped in tradition and history.

Stella Melissa

CHAPTER 5: GETTING AROUND SCOTLAND

Navigating the rugged and scenic landscapes of Scotland is an adventure in itself. Whether you're traversing the highlands, exploring coastal paths, or venturing into remote islands, understanding your transportation options and planning your routes will enhance your hiking experience. In this chapter, we will explore the various modes of transportation available in Scotland, offer guidance on navigating hiking trails, provide tips and regulations for driving in Scotland, and suggest recommended hiking itineraries for different trip durations.

Transportation Options

Buses

Buses are a convenient and cost-effective way to travel across Scotland, connecting major cities, towns, and rural areas.

Intercity Buses:
- Operators: Major operators include Citylink, Stagecoach, and Megabus.
- Routes: These services connect cities like Edinburgh, Glasgow, Inverness, and Aberdeen.
- Booking: Tickets can be booked online through the operators' websites or at bus stations.
- Frequency: Buses run frequently between major cities, with reduced services on weekends and holidays.

Regional and Local Buses:
- Operators: Local operators vary by region.

Stella Melissa

- Routes: These buses connect smaller towns and rural areas.
- Schedules: Timetables can be found on the operators' websites or local tourist information centers.
- Fares: Fares are usually paid to the driver in cash or contactless payment.

Tips for Bus Travel:
- Plan Ahead: Check timetables and routes in advance.
- Contactless Payments: Many buses accept contactless payments for added convenience.
- Local Advice: Ask locals or tourist information centers for bus route recommendations.

Trains

Scotland's rail network offers scenic journeys through the countryside, connecting major cities and remote areas.

Main Train Operators:

Scotland Hiking Guidebook

- ScotRail: The primary train operator in Scotland, providing services across the country.
- LNER: Provides services from London to Edinburgh and beyond.
- Caledonian Sleeper: Overnight services from London to various Scottish destinations.

Key Routes:
- West Highland Line: Glasgow to Mallaig, passing through breathtaking highland scenery.
- East Coast Main Line: Connects Edinburgh to London, with stops in major cities.
- Kyle Line: Inverness to Kyle of Lochalsh, offering stunning views of the highlands.

Booking and Tickets:
- Online Booking: Tickets can be booked on the ScotRail website, Trainline, or other booking platforms.
- Rail Passes: Consider the Spirit of Scotland Travelpass or BritRail Pass for unlimited travel options.

Tips for Train Travel:

- Advance Booking: Book tickets in advance for better fares and seat reservations.
- Scenic Routes: Take advantage of Scotland's scenic railways for a unique travel experience.
- Facilities: Trains offer amenities such as Wi-Fi, dining cars, and luggage space.

Car Rentals

Renting a car gives you the flexibility to explore Scotland at your own pace, especially in remote and rural areas.

Major Car Rental Companies:
- Avis, Hertz, Enterprise, Sixt: Available in major cities and airports.
- Arnold Clark: A Scottish car rental company with various locations.

Requirements:

- Driving License: A valid driving license is required. International visitors may need an International Driving Permit.
- Age Restrictions: Drivers must be at least 21 years old, with additional fees for drivers under 25.
- Insurance: Ensure adequate insurance coverage, including collision damage waiver and theft protection.

Booking and Picking Up:
- Online Booking: Book online through the rental company's website or comparison sites.
- Pick-Up Locations: Cars can be picked up at airports, city centers, and rental offices.

Tips for Car Rentals:
- Fuel Policy: Check the fuel policy (full-to-full or pre-purchase).
- Navigation: Consider renting a GPS device or using navigation apps.
- Inspect the Car: Check for any damages before driving off and report them to the rental company.

Stella Melissa

Ferries

Ferries are essential for reaching Scotland's many islands, offering a scenic way to travel.

Major Ferry Operators:
- Caledonian MacBrayne (CalMac): Operates services to the Hebrides and other islands.
- NorthLink Ferries: Connects mainland Scotland with Orkney and Shetland.
- Pentland Ferries: Offers services to Orkney.

Key Routes:
- Hebrides: Ferries from Oban, Mallaig, and Ullapool to islands like Skye, Mull, and Harris.
- Orkney and Shetland: Services from Aberdeen, Scrabster, and Gills Bay.

Booking and Tickets:
- Online Booking: Book tickets on the ferry operators' websites.

- Advance Booking: Recommended during peak seasons and holidays.

Tips for Ferry Travel:
- Check Schedules: Ferry schedules can be affected by weather conditions.
- Vehicle Reservations: If traveling with a vehicle, book in advance.
- Facilities: Ferries offer amenities such as dining areas, lounges, and cabins.

Navigating Hiking Trails: Maps and Apps

Traditional Maps

OS Maps
- Ordnance Survey (OS) Maps: The most detailed and reliable maps for hiking in Scotland.
- Types: Explorer series (1:25,000 scale) and Landranger series (1:50,000 scale).
- Availability: Purchase at outdoor shops, bookstores, or online.

Stella Melissa

Tips for Using Maps:

- Familiarize Yourself: Learn to read contour lines, symbols, and grid references.

- Weather Protection: Use a map case to protect your map from rain and wind.

- Compass: Carry a compass and know how to use it in conjunction with your map.

Digital Maps and Apps

ViewRanger

- Overview: A popular app for hikers, offering detailed maps and route planning.

- Features: Offline maps, GPS tracking, route sharing, and safety alerts.

- Availability: Downloadable from the App Store and Google Play.

OS Maps App

- Overview: The digital version of Ordnance Survey maps.

- Features: Access to all OS Explorer and Landranger maps, route planning, and GPS navigation.
- Availability: Subscription-based, available on the App Store and Google Play.

AllTrails

- Overview: An app with a large database of trails, user reviews, and photos.
- Features: Trail maps, GPS tracking, and offline map capabilities.
- Availability: Free and premium versions available on the App Store and Google Play.

Tips for Using Apps:
- Download Maps: Ensure maps are downloaded for offline use in areas with poor signal.
- Battery Life: Carry a portable charger to keep your device powered.
- Safety Features: Utilize safety features such as route sharing and location tracking.

Stella Melissa

Driving in Scotland: Tips and Regulations

Driving Regulations

General Rules:
- Drive on the Left: In Scotland, vehicles drive on the left side of the road.
- Speed Limits: Vary by road type—30 mph in built-up areas, 60 mph on single carriageways, and 70 mph on dual carriageways and motorways.
- Seat Belts: Mandatory for all passengers.
- Drink-Driving: Strict limits apply; the legal limit is lower than in many other countries.

Documentation:
- Driving License: Carry your driving license at all times.
- Insurance: Ensure you have adequate insurance coverage.
- MOT and Tax: Vehicles must be roadworthy and display valid tax and MOT.

Road Types and Conditions

Motorways and Dual Carriageways
- Description: Fast, multi-lane roads connecting major cities.
- Speed Limits: 70 mph.
- Tips: Stay in the left lane unless overtaking, use designated exits.

A Roads
- Description: Primary routes connecting towns and cities, often single carriageways.
- Speed Limits: 60 mph.
- Tips: Be cautious of slower traffic and frequent junctions.

B Roads and Minor Roads
- Description: Secondary roads, often narrow and winding.
- Speed Limits: 60 mph, but adjust speed according to conditions.

- Tips: Watch for oncoming traffic, livestock, and pedestrians.

Single Track Roads
- Description: Narrow roads with passing places, common in rural and highland areas.
- Speed Limits: 60 mph, but often driven slower.
- Tips: Use passing places to allow oncoming traffic to pass, and be prepared to reverse if necessary.

Driving Tips

Navigating the Highlands
- Weather: Be prepared for sudden changes in weather, including fog and rain.
- Wildlife: Watch for deer and other wildlife, especially at dawn and dusk.
- Fuel: Fill up at major towns as fuel stations can be sparse in remote areas.

Parking

Scotland Hiking Guidebook

- Cities: Use designated parking lots or on-street parking; check for restrictions and fees.
- Rural Areas: Use designated parking areas at trailheads and scenic spots.

Emergency Numbers:
- General Emergency: Dial 999 or 112.
- Breakdown Assistance: Consider joining a breakdown service like AA or RAC for peace of mind.

Recommended Hiking Itineraries

1-Week Itinerary

Day 1: Edinburgh
- Overview: Start in the capital city, exploring its historical sites and nearby hills.
- Activities: Visit Edinburgh Castle, hike up Arthur's Seat for panoramic views.
- Accommodation: Stay in a central hotel like the Radisson Blu Hotel (80 High St, Edinburgh, EH1 1TH).

Stella Melissa

Day 2: Loch Lomond and The Trossachs
- Overview: Head to this national park known for its lochs and mountains.
- Activities: Hike the Ben A'an trail for stunning views.
- Accommodation: Camp or stay at a lodge like The Winnock Hotel (The Square, Drymen, Glasgow G63 0BL).

Day 3: Glencoe
- Overview: Explore the dramatic landscapes of Glencoe.
- Activities: Hike the Lost Valley trail, visit Glencoe Visitor Centre.
- Accommodation: Stay at Clachaig Inn (Glencoe, Ballachulish PH49 4HX).

Day 4: Isle of Skye
- Overview: Drive to the Isle of Skye, famous for its rugged scenery.
- Activities: Hike the Old Man of Storr, explore Fairy Pools.
- Accommodation: Stay at Sligachan Hotel (Sligachan, Isle of Skye IV47 8SW).

Day 5: Fort William and Ben Nevis

- Overview: Visit Fort William, the gateway to Ben Nevis.
- Activities: Hike to the summit of Ben Nevis, the UK's highest peak.
- Accommodation: Stay at Ben Nevis Hotel & Leisure Club (North Rd, Fort William PH33 6TG).

Day 6: Cairngorms National Park

- Overview: Explore the largest national park in the UK.
- Activities: Hike the Cairngorm Mountain trails, visit Aviemore.
- Accommodation: Stay at The Boat Hotel (Deshar Rd, Boat of Garten PH24 3BH).

Day 7: Inverness and Loch Ness

- Overview: Finish your trip in Inverness, with a visit to Loch Ness.
- Activities: Hike the South Loch Ness Trail, visit Urquhart Castle.
- Accommodation: Stay at Kingsmills Hotel (Culcabock Rd, Inverness IV2 3LP).

Stella Melissa

2-Week Itinerary

Week 1: Follow the 1-Week Itinerary

Week 2: Additional Destinations

Day 8: Outer Hebrides
- Overview: Take a ferry to the Outer Hebrides.
- Activities: Hike the Hebridean Way, explore Harris and Lewis.
- Accommodation: Stay at Hotel Hebrides (Pier Rd, Tarbert, Isle of Harris HS3 3DG).

Day 9: Isle of Mull
- Overview: Travel to the Isle of Mull.
- Activities: Hike to the top of Ben More, visit Tobermory.
- Accommodation: Stay at Tobermory Hotel (Main St, Tobermory, Isle of Mull PA75 6NT).

Day 10: Oban
- Overview: Return to the mainland, visiting Oban.

- Activities: Explore the town, hike to McCaig's Tower.
- Accommodation: Stay at The Perle Oban Hotel (Station Square, Oban PA34 5RT).

Day 11: Loch Ness and Great Glen Way
- Overview: Walk part of the Great Glen Way.
- Activities: Hike from Fort Augustus to Drumnadrochit.
- Accommodation: Stay at Loch Ness Lodge (Brachla, Inverness IV3 8LA).

Day 12: Speyside Way
- Overview: Explore the Speyside region, known for its whisky distilleries.
- Activities: Hike the Speyside Way, visit a distillery.
- Accommodation: Stay at The Station Hotel (51 New St, Rothes, Aberlour AB38 7BJ).

Day 13: Perthshire
- Overview: Head to Perthshire, known for its forests and hills.
- Activities: Hike in The Hermitage, visit Dunkeld.

Stella Melissa

- Accommodation: Stay at Dunkeld House Hotel (Dunkeld, Perthshire PH8 0HX).

Day 14: St Andrews and East Neuk of Fife
- Overview: Conclude your trip in the charming town of St Andrews and the coastal villages of East Neuk.
- Activities: Walk the Fife Coastal Path, visit St Andrews Cathedral.
- Accommodation: Stay at Hotel du Vin St Andrews (40 The Scores, St Andrews KY16 9AS).

Weekend Getaway Itinerary

Day 1: Edinburgh to Glencoe
- Morning: Travel from Edinburgh to Glencoe (approx. 2.5 hours by car).
- Afternoon: Hike the Lost Valley trail.
- Evening: Stay at Clachaig Inn (Glencoe, Ballachulish PH49 4HX).

Day 2: Glencoe to Isle of Skye

Scotland Hiking Guidebook

- Morning: Drive to the Isle of Skye (approx. 2 hours by car).
- Afternoon: Hike the Old Man of Storr.
- Evening: Stay at Sligachan Hotel (Sligachan, Isle of Skye IV47 8SW).

Day 3: Isle of Skye to Edinburgh
- Morning: Explore the Fairy Pools.
- Afternoon: Drive back to Edinburgh (approx. 5.5 hours by car).

Getting around Scotland to explore its diverse hiking trails requires a mix of planning and flexibility. Whether you choose to travel by bus, train, car, or ferry, each mode of transportation offers unique advantages and opportunities to experience the country's stunning landscapes. Equipped with maps, apps, and knowledge of driving regulations, you can confidently navigate Scotland's trails. Our recommended itineraries provide a starting point for your adventure, ensuring you make the most of your time in this breathtaking country. Embrace the journey, discover hidden gems, and immerse yourself

Stella Melissa

in the natural beauty and rich culture that Scotland has to offer.

Scotland Hiking Guidebook

CHAPTER 6: FOOD AND DRINK

Introduction to Scottish Cuisine

Scotland, with its rugged landscapes and rich cultural heritage, boasts a culinary tradition that is both hearty and flavorful. Scottish cuisine is deeply rooted in its natural environment, with a focus on locally sourced ingredients, from the abundant seafood caught off its coasts to the game and livestock raised in its pastures. The country's culinary history has been influenced by its geography, climate, and historical events, creating a unique blend of flavors and dishes that reflect its diverse regions.

Historical Influence on Scottish Cuisine

Scottish cuisine has evolved over centuries, influenced by its Celtic, Norse, and English neighbors. The ancient Scots relied on what they could hunt, gather, and farm, leading to a diet rich in game, fish, berries, and root vegetables. The introduction of new crops and spices through trade and colonization expanded the Scottish palate, incorporating ingredients such as potatoes, sugar, and tea.

Contemporary Scottish Cuisine

Modern Scottish cuisine continues to celebrate its traditional roots while embracing contemporary culinary techniques. Today, Scotland is home to numerous award-winning restaurants and chefs who take pride in showcasing the best of Scottish produce. From Michelin-starred dining establishments to cozy local eateries, there is no shortage of places to savor the flavors of Scotland.

Must-Try Dishes and Local Specialties

Scotland's culinary repertoire includes a variety of dishes that are synonymous with its culture and heritage. When hiking through Scotland, you'll have the opportunity to sample these must-try dishes and local specialties.

Haggis:

Overview: Perhaps the most iconic of all Scottish dishes, haggis is a savory pudding made from sheep's offal (heart, liver, and lungs) mixed with oats, onions, and spices, traditionally encased in a sheep's stomach.

Serving: Often served with "neeps and tatties" (mashed turnips and potatoes) and a dram of whisky, haggis is a staple at Burns Night suppers and other Scottish celebrations.

Cullen Skink:

Stella Melissa

Overview: This hearty soup hails from the fishing village of Cullen in northeastern Scotland. Made with smoked haddock, potatoes, onions, and milk or cream, Cullen skink is a comforting dish that warms the soul.

Serving: Enjoy it as a starter or a light meal, often accompanied by crusty bread.

Scotch Pie:

Overview: A popular snack or lunch item, Scotch pies are small, double-crust meat pies filled with minced mutton or other meats, seasoned with spices.

Serving: Typically enjoyed hot, Scotch pies are a common sight at football matches and local bakeries.

Cranachan:

Overview: A traditional Scottish dessert, cranachan is made from whipped cream, honey, whisky, toasted oats, and fresh raspberries.

Serving: Often served in individual glasses, it is a delightful end to any meal, celebrating the best of Scotland's dairy and berry produce.

Arbroath Smokie:
Overview: This smoked haddock delicacy originates from the town of Arbroath. The fish is traditionally cured in salt overnight before being hot-smoked over a hardwood fire.

Serving: Enjoy Arbroath smokies hot or cold, often paired with buttered bread or added to soups and stews.

Black Pudding:
Overview: Black pudding is a type of blood sausage made with pork blood, fat, and oatmeal. It is a staple of the traditional Scottish breakfast.

Serving: Often fried or grilled, black pudding can be enjoyed on its own or as part of a full Scottish breakfast.

Shortbread:

Overview: A beloved Scottish treat, shortbread is a simple yet delicious biscuit made from butter, sugar, and flour.

Serving: Perfect with a cup of tea, shortbread is also a popular gift and can be found in various shapes and flavors.

Best Places to Eat and Drink on Your Hike

Scotland's hiking trails not only offer stunning landscapes but also opportunities to indulge in delicious food and drink. Here are some of the best places to eat and drink while exploring the country's trails.

The Bothy Bistro, Burghead:

Location: 16 Grant Street, Burghead, IV30 5UE

Overview: Located near the Moray Coast Trail, The Bothy Bistro offers a cozy atmosphere and a menu featuring fresh, locally sourced seafood and seasonal produce.

Specialties: Try their Cullen skink, fish and chips, and homemade desserts.

The Clachaig Inn, Glencoe:
Location: Glencoe, Ballachulish, PH49 4HX

Overview: Nestled in the heart of Glencoe, The Clachaig Inn is a favorite among hikers and climbers. It offers hearty meals, real ales, and stunning views of the surrounding mountains.

Specialties: Enjoy their venison burger, haggis, and extensive selection of whiskies.

Applecross Inn, Applecross:
Location: Shore Street, Applecross, IV54 8LR

Stella Melissa

Overview: Situated on the remote Applecross Peninsula, this inn is a gem for hikers exploring the area. It is renowned for its fresh seafood and welcoming ambiance.

Specialties: Don't miss their langoustines, scallops, and seafood chowder.

The Drovers Inn, Inverarnan:
Location: Inverarnan, Arrochar, G83 7DX

Overview: A historic inn dating back to 1705, The Drovers Inn is located along the West Highland Way. It offers traditional Scottish fare and a rustic atmosphere.

Specialties: Try their steak and ale pie, haggis, and sticky toffee pudding.

Glenfinnan House Hotel, Glenfinnan:
Location: Glenfinnan, PH37 4LT

Overview: Overlooking Loch Shiel and the Glenfinnan Viaduct, this hotel offers a serene dining experience with a focus on local ingredients.

Specialties: Enjoy their Highland venison, seafood platter, and cranachan.

The Real Food Café, Tyndrum:
Location: A82, Tyndrum, FK20 8RY

Overview: A popular stop for hikers on the West Highland Way, The Real Food Café serves delicious comfort food, including fish and chips and homemade soups.

Specialties: Their award-winning fish and chips and vegetarian haggis are must-tries.

Stella Melissa

Food Markets and Culinary Tours

Exploring local food markets and participating in culinary tours can enhance your understanding and appreciation of Scottish cuisine.

Edinburgh Farmers' Market:
Location: Castle Terrace, Edinburgh, EH1 2EN

Overview: Held every Saturday, the Edinburgh Farmers' Market offers a wide range of local produce, artisanal products, and freshly prepared foods.

Highlights: Sample Scottish cheeses, smoked salmon, and homemade preserves.

Glasgow's Barras Market:
Location: Moncur Street, Glasgow, G40 2SB

Overview: A bustling market in the East End of Glasgow, the Barras Market features an eclectic mix of food stalls, antiques, and crafts.

Highlights: Enjoy street food, fresh produce, and unique culinary finds.

Inverness Victorian Market:

Location: Academy Street, Inverness, IV1 1JN

Overview: This historic market offers a variety of food stalls, local crafts, and specialty shops in a charming Victorian setting.

Highlights: Try local delicacies, freshly baked goods, and handmade chocolates.

The Stockbridge Market, Edinburgh:

Location: Saunders Street, Edinburgh, EH3 6TQ

Overview: Open every Sunday, the Stockbridge Market is a favorite among locals and visitors for its selection of artisanal foods and crafts.

Highlights: Sample gourmet street food, artisanal cheeses, and organic produce.

Stella Melissa

Culinary Tours

Eat Walk Edinburgh
Overview: This guided food tour takes you through the heart of Edinburgh, offering tastings at various restaurants, pubs, and specialty shops.

Highlights: Enjoy samples of haggis, Scottish cheese, and whisky while learning about the city's culinary history.

Glasgow Food and Drink Tour:
Overview: Explore Glasgow's vibrant food scene with a guided tour that includes stops at local eateries, markets, and bars.

Highlights: Taste traditional Scottish dishes, craft beers, and local spirits.

Highland Food Safari:

Scotland Hiking Guidebook

Overview: Discover the culinary delights of the Scottish Highlands with a guided tour that includes visits to local producers, farms, and distilleries.

Highlights: Enjoy tastings of Highland beef, smoked salmon, and whisky, while learning about the region's food heritage.

Traditional Pubs and Whisky Trails

No trip to Scotland is complete without experiencing its traditional pubs and whisky trails. These establishments offer a glimpse into the country's social and cultural fabric, where you can enjoy hearty meals, local brews, and the finest Scotch whiskies.

Traditional Pubs

The Sheep Heid Inn, Edinburgh:
Location: 43-45 The Causeway, Edinburgh, EH15 3QA

Stella Melissa

Overview: One of Scotland's oldest pubs, dating back to 1360, The Sheep Heid Inn offers a cozy atmosphere, traditional pub fare, and a selection of local ales and whiskies.

Specialties: Try their steak and ale pie, fish and chips, and selection of single malts.

The Drovers Inn, Inverarnan:
Location: Inverarnan, Arrochar, G83 7DX

Overview: As mentioned earlier, this historic inn along the West Highland Way is known for its rustic charm and hearty Scottish dishes.

Specialties: Enjoy their haggis, venison stew, and extensive whisky collection.

The Clachaig Inn, Glencoe:
Location: Glencoe, Ballachulish, PH49 4HX

Scotland Hiking Guidebook

Overview: A favorite among hikers and climbers, The Clachaig Inn offers a warm welcome, hearty meals, and a selection of real ales and whiskies.

Specialties: Don't miss their game pie, venison burger, and whisky tasting flights.

Whisky Trails

Scotland is renowned for its whisky production, and exploring whisky distilleries along designated whisky trails is a must for enthusiasts and casual drinkers alike.

Speyside Whisky Trail:
Overview: Located in the heart of whisky country, Speyside is home to the highest concentration of distilleries in Scotland. The trail winds through picturesque landscapes and historic towns, offering visitors the opportunity to tour world-famous distilleries such as Glenfiddich, Glenlivet, and Macallan.

Stella Melissa

Highlights: Experience guided tours, tastings of single malt Scotch whiskies, and learn about the whisky-making process from expert distillers.

Islay Whisky Trail:

Overview: Islay, known for its distinctive peaty whiskies, offers a unique whisky trail experience. Visit renowned distilleries like Laphroaig, Ardbeg, and Lagavulin, nestled among rugged coastal scenery and ancient ruins.

Highlights: Discover the smoky flavors of Islay whiskies, explore traditional distilling techniques, and enjoy scenic views of the Atlantic Ocean.

Highland Whisky Trail:

Overview: The Highland region boasts a diverse range of whisky distilleries, each with its own character and style. From the historic Glen Ord Distillery near Inverness to the scenic Dalwhinnie Distillery in the Cairngorms National Park, the Highland Whisky Trail offers a journey through Scotland's rich whisky heritage.

Highlights: Tour distilleries set against stunning Highland landscapes, sample Highland single malts, and learn about the region's role in shaping Scotch whisky history.

Tips for Enjoying Scottish Food and Drink

1. Try Local: Embrace the opportunity to sample local specialties and dishes that highlight Scotland's natural bounty, from seafood along the coast to game meats from the Highlands.

2. Pairing with Whisky: Scottish cuisine pairs exceptionally well with Scotch whisky. Experiment with different whisky styles to complement your meals, whether enjoying a dram with haggis or seafood.

3. Seasonal Delights: Scotland's cuisine varies with the seasons, offering fresh produce and seasonal specialties. Plan your culinary experiences around local festivals and events celebrating food and drink.

4. Pub Culture: Visit traditional pubs not only for their food and drink but also for their lively atmosphere and sense of community. Pubs often serve as gathering places where locals and visitors alike share stories and enjoy music.

5. Respect Local Customs: When dining out or visiting pubs, observe local customs and etiquette. Tipping practices may vary, and table manners reflect Scottish hospitality and tradition.

6. Culinary Events: Keep an eye out for culinary events and food festivals throughout Scotland. These events offer opportunities to taste a wide range of dishes, meet local producers, and participate in cooking demonstrations.

Exploring Scotland's food and drink scene while hiking its breathtaking trails offers a sensory journey through the country's rich cultural heritage and natural landscapes. From savoring traditional dishes like haggis and Cullen skink to sampling the finest Scotch whiskies along whisky trails, every culinary experience in Scotland is infused with history, tradition, and a deep connection to the land. Whether you're enjoying a hearty meal in a cozy pub or discovering local flavors at a food market, let Scotland's cuisine enhance your hiking adventure and leave you with lasting memories of this remarkable country.

CHAPTER 7: PRACTICAL INFORMATION AND TRAVEL TIPS

Internet and Communication

Staying connected while hiking in Scotland can enhance your experience by allowing you to share your adventures in real-time, access maps and trail information, and stay in touch with loved ones. Here's what you need to know about internet and communication in Scotland:

1. Mobile Coverage: Mobile phone coverage in Scotland varies depending on your location. Urban areas and towns generally have good 4G coverage, while rural and remote areas, especially in the Highlands and islands, may have limited or no signal. Major mobile networks in Scotland include EE, O2, Vodafone, and Three.

2. SIM Cards: If you're visiting from abroad, consider purchasing a local SIM card for your phone. These are readily available at airports, convenience stores, and mobile shops. A local SIM card will give you access to local rates for calls, texts, and data.

3. Wi-Fi: Free Wi-Fi is commonly available in cafes, restaurants, hotels, and public spaces in towns and cities. Many accommodations, including guesthouses and hostels, offer free Wi-Fi to guests. For more remote areas, consider downloading offline maps and guides in advance.

4. Communication Apps: Apps like WhatsApp, Skype, and FaceTime are popular for staying in touch with

friends and family. Ensure you have these installed and set up before your trip.

5. Emergency Numbers: In case of emergencies, dial 999 or 112 to reach emergency services (police, fire, ambulance, and mountain rescue). It's wise to save these numbers in your phone and familiarize yourself with your location's nearest medical facilities.

Money Matters: Currency, ATMs, and Tipping

Understanding the financial aspects of traveling in Scotland will help you manage your budget and avoid any monetary mishaps. Here are some key points:

1. Currency: The currency used in Scotland is the Pound Sterling (£). Banknotes and coins come in various denominations, with the most common banknotes being £5, £10, £20, and £50.

2. ATMs: ATMs (known as cash machines in the UK) are widely available in towns, cities, and larger villages. Most ATMs accept international cards, but check with your bank about any fees that may apply for overseas withdrawals. It's a good idea to carry some cash, especially in remote areas where card payments might not be accepted.

3. Credit and Debit Cards: Credit and debit cards are widely accepted throughout Scotland. Visa and MasterCard are the most commonly accepted, while American Express may not be accepted everywhere. Contactless payment is also prevalent.

4. Tipping: Tipping in Scotland is generally not obligatory but is appreciated for good service. In restaurants, a tip of 10-15% of the bill is customary if service is not already included. For taxi drivers, rounding up the fare or adding a small amount is typical. Hotel staff, such as porters and housekeeping, may also be tipped a few pounds for good service.

5. Currency Exchange: Currency exchange services are available at airports, banks, and dedicated currency exchange offices. Rates may vary, so it's worth shopping around for the best deal. Using ATMs for withdrawals can often provide a better exchange rate compared to exchange bureaus.

Local Etiquette

Understanding and respecting local customs and etiquette will enhance your experience and ensure positive interactions with locals. Here are some guidelines to keep in mind:

1. Politeness and Greetings: Scots are generally polite and appreciate good manners. Greetings like "hello," "please," and "thank you" are important. In rural areas, it's customary to greet fellow hikers with a friendly nod or hello.

2. Queueing: The British, including Scots, value orderly queueing. Always wait your turn in lines and avoid cutting in.

3. Punctuality: Being on time is appreciated, especially for formal events, reservations, and appointments.

4. Respecting Privacy: Scots value their privacy. Avoid intrusive questions or topics, and respect personal space.

5. Dress Code: Casual attire is acceptable in most settings, but some restaurants and venues may have a smart-casual dress code. When hiking, appropriate outdoor clothing and sturdy footwear are essential.

6. Wildlife and Nature: Respect wildlife and natural habitats. Avoid disturbing animals, and leave no trace by taking your litter with you. Stick to designated paths to protect the environment.

Stella Melissa

Sustainable and Responsible Hiking

Scotland's natural beauty is a treasure that must be preserved for future generations. Sustainable and responsible hiking practices are crucial in maintaining the health of the environment and local communities. Here are some tips:

1. Leave No Trace: Follow the Leave No Trace principles by minimizing your impact on the environment. Pack out all litter, including biodegradable items, and avoid damaging plants and wildlife.

2. Stick to Paths: Stay on marked trails to prevent erosion and protect fragile ecosystems. Avoid creating new paths, as this can harm the environment.

3. Respect Wildlife: Observe animals from a distance and avoid feeding them. Disturbing wildlife can have negative effects on their natural behavior and health.

4. Use Reusable Items: Reduce waste by using reusable water bottles, containers, and utensils. Avoid single-use plastics whenever possible.

5. Camp Responsibly: If wild camping, choose a site at least 100 meters from roads, buildings, and water sources. Follow the Scottish Outdoor Access Code, which provides guidelines for responsible camping and land use.

6. Support Local Communities: Buy local products, eat at local restaurants, and stay in locally-owned accommodations to support the economy. Respect local customs and traditions.

7. Transport Choices: Use public transport, carpool, or hike to reduce your carbon footprint. Consider eco-friendly options like electric vehicle rentals or bike hire.

Essential Gear and Packing Checklist

Packing the right gear is essential for a safe and enjoyable hiking experience in Scotland. Here's a comprehensive checklist to ensure you're well-prepared:

1. Clothing:
   - Waterproof jacket and trousers
   - Insulating layers (fleece or down jacket)
   - Base layers (moisture-wicking shirts and thermal leggings)
   - Sturdy hiking boots with good ankle support
   - Comfortable hiking socks (preferably wool or synthetic)
   - Hat, gloves, and scarf for colder weather
   - Sun hat and sunglasses for sunny days
   - Gaiters (optional, for muddy or wet conditions)

2. Navigation and Safety:
   - Detailed map of the hiking area (OS maps are recommended)
   - Compass and GPS device

Scotland Hiking Guidebook

 - Fully charged mobile phone with emergency contacts saved
 - First aid kit (including blister treatment and personal medications)
 - Emergency whistle and signal mirror
 - Headlamp or flashlight with extra batteries
 - Multi-tool or Swiss Army knife

3. Food and Hydration:
 - Reusable water bottles or hydration system (2-3 liters capacity)
 - Water purification tablets or filter (for longer hikes)
 - High-energy snacks (nuts, dried fruit, energy bars)
 - Packed lunch (sandwiches, wraps, or other portable meals)
 - Lightweight stove and cookware (for multi-day hikes)
 - Reusable utensils and containers

4. Camping Gear (for multi-day hikes):
 - Lightweight tent or bivvy bag
 - Sleeping bag suitable for the season

Stella Melissa

- Sleeping pad for insulation and comfort
- Stove, fuel, and lighter/matches
- Cooking pot and utensils
- Biodegradable soap and sponge for cleaning

5. Miscellaneous Items:

- Backpack with rain cover (20-40 liters for day hikes, 40-70 liters for multi-day hikes)
- Trekking poles (optional, but useful for stability)
- Dry bags or waterproof sacks for gear protection
- Personal identification and necessary permits
- Cash and bank cards
- Camera or smartphone for capturing memories
- Guidebook or notes (for trail information and inspiration)

By preparing thoroughly and respecting the environment and local customs, you can ensure a safe, enjoyable, and memorable hiking experience in Scotland. As you venture through the country's stunning landscapes and immerse yourself in its rich history and culture, you'll create lasting memories and a deeper appreciation for this remarkable destination.

Stella Melissa

APPENDICES

15 FAQs About Hiking in Scotland

1. **What is the best time to go hiking in Scotland?** The best time for hiking depends on your preferences. Spring (May-June) offers pleasant temperatures and wildflowers, while summer (July-August) provides longer daylight hours but can be more crowded. Autumn (September-October) boasts stunning fall foliage, but be prepared for changeable weather. Winter hiking requires proper gear and experience due to snow and ice.

2. **What are the different types of hikes available in Scotland?** Scotland offers a variety of hikes, from short, family-friendly nature trails to challenging multi-day treks. Popular options include Munro bagging (climbing Scotland's mountains over 3,000 ft), coastal hikes, loch (lake) trails, and historic walks.

3. **Do I need a permit to hike in Scotland?** Permits are generally not required for day hikes on most trails.

However, some specific routes or activities might have restrictions. It's always best to check with the landowner or relevant authority beforehand.

4. **What kind of navigation skills do I need for hiking in Scotland?** Even on well-marked trails, a basic understanding of navigation is crucial. Being able to read a map and compass and knowing how to use a GPS device can be very helpful, especially in case of bad weather or getting lost.

5. **What safety gear should I bring hiking in Scotland?** Proper footwear with good ankle support is essential. Pack weather-appropriate clothing (layers), a waterproof jacket, a hat, gloves, and a map and compass. Consider bringing a first-aid kit, whistle, and emergency shelter depending on the difficulty of the hike.

6. **What are the Scottish Outdoor Access Code guidelines?** The Scottish Outdoor Access Code promotes responsible enjoyment of the outdoors. Respect the land, wildlife, and other people you

encounter. Leave no trace, stick to designated paths, and close gates behind you.

7. **Are there any guided hikes available?** Yes, many companies offer guided hikes in Scotland, catering to various experience levels and interests. This can be a good option for exploring lesser-known trails or learning more about the local history and environment.

8. **What kind of wildlife can I see while hiking in Scotland?** Keep an eye out for red deer, golden eagles, wildcats, and a variety of bird species. Be mindful of wildlife and maintain a safe distance.

9. **Are there any midges in Scotland?** Midges are tiny flying insects that can be a nuisance during the summer months, particularly in damp areas. Consider insect repellent and head netting for additional comfort.

10. **What are the typical food and drink options on hiking trails?** There are limited food and drink options

on most trails. Pack plenty of water and snacks to fuel your hike.

11. **What are the restroom facilities like on hiking trails?** Restrooms are not readily available on most trails. Plan accordingly and utilize designated restroom areas when available.

12. **Can I bring my dog hiking in Scotland?** Dogs are generally welcome on trails in Scotland, but be sure to keep them leashed and clean up after them. Always check for any restrictions on specific trails.

13. **What is the mobile phone network coverage like in remote areas?** Mobile phone reception can be limited in some parts of Scotland, particularly in the highlands and on remote trails. Don't rely solely on your phone for navigation.

14. **What currency is used in Scotland?** The official currency in Scotland is the British Pound Sterling (£).

15. **What are some tips for minimizing my impact on the environment while hiking?** Follow Leave No Trace principles. Pack out all trash, avoid disturbing wildlife, and stick to designated paths to minimize erosion.

15 Fun Facts About Scotland

1. Scotland is a part of the United Kingdom but has its own distinct parliament, flag, and culture.
2. Scotland is home to over 790 islands, including the famous Isle of Skye and the Outer Hebrides.
3. The Loch Ness monster, affectionately nicknamed "Nessie," is a mythical creature said to inhabit Loch Ness, Scotland's largest freshwater lake by volume.
4. Kilt, the famous Scottish garment, is a pleated tartan skirt traditionally worn by men.
5. Bagpipes are the national instrument of Scotland and are a prominent feature in traditional music.
6. Edinburgh, Scotland's capital city, is known for its historic castle and medieval Old Town.
7. Scotland is the birthplace of golf, with the Old Course at St Andrews considered the "Home of Golf."

8. The Scottish Highlands offer stunning mountain ranges, including Ben Nevis, the highest peak in the British Isles.
9. Scotland has a rich literary heritage, being the birthplace of famous authors like Sir Walter Scott and J.K. Rowling.
10. Haggis, a savory dish made from sheep's heart, liver, and lungs, is a traditional Scottish food.
11. The ancient stone circles of Callanish on the Isle of Lewis are a prehistoric monument older than Stonehenge.
12. Scotland is famous for its whisky production, with distilleries scattered throughout the country.
13. The game of curling, similar to shuffleboard played on ice, is a popular winter sport in Scotland.
14. Many castles dot the Scottish landscape, remnants of a turbulent past and offering a glimpse into history.
15. The Edinburgh Festival Fringe, the world's largest arts festival, takes place annually in Edinburgh.

Stella Melissa

Emergency Contacts and Useful Links

- **Scottish Emergency Services:** 999
- **Mountain Rescue:** (UK-wide) 0913 662 552
- **NHS 24 (National Health Service)**: 111
- **Police Scotland:** 101

Useful Links:

- VisitScotland: https://www.visitscotland.com/
- Scottish Outdoor Access Code: https://www.outdooraccess-scotland.scot/
- Mountaineering Scotland: https://www.mountaineering.scot/
- Met Office - Scotland Weather: https://www.metoffice.gov.uk/

By familiarizing yourself with these emergency contacts and resources, you can ensure a safe and enjoyable hiking adventure in the beautiful landscapes of Scotland.

Scotland Hiking Guidebook

MAP OF SCOTTISH HIGHLAND

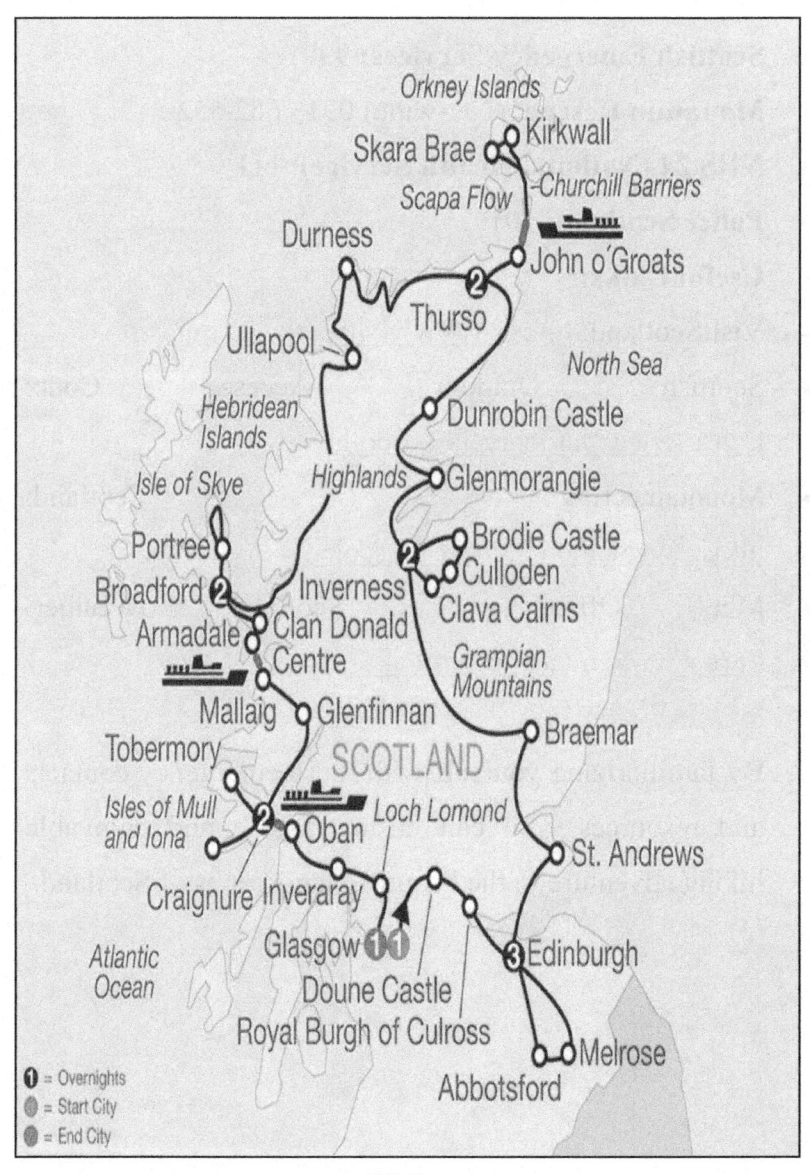

Orkney Islands
Kirkwall
Skara Brae
Scapa Flow
Churchill Barriers
Durness
John o'Groats
Thurso
Ullapool
North Sea
Hebridean Islands
Dunrobin Castle
Isle of Skye
Highlands
Glenmorangie
Portree
Brodie Castle
Broadford
Culloden
Inverness
Armadale
Clan Donald Centre
Clava Cairns
Grampian Mountains
Mallaig
Glenfinnan
Tobermory
Braemar
SCOTLAND
Isles of Mull and Iona
Loch Lomond
Oban
St. Andrews
Craignure Inveraray
Atlantic Ocean
Glasgow
Edinburgh
Doune Castle
Royal Burgh of Culross
Melrose
Abbotsford

❶ = Overnights
◯ = Start City
◯ = End City

122

Made in the USA
Monee, IL
20 December 2024